QUICK EXPERT'S GUIDE

Build Your Own Web Site

Chris Martin

ROSEN
PUBLISHING®

New York

Published in 2014 by The Rosen Publishing Group, Inc.
29 East 21st Street, New York, NY 10010

Senior editor: Julia Adams
Design: Rocket Design (East Anglia) Ltd
All images and graphic elements: Shutterstock

Library of Congress Cataloging-in-Publication Data

Martin, Chris, 1967– author.
Build your own web site/Chris Martin.—First edition.
    pages cm.—(Quick expert's guide)
Audience: Grade 5 to 7.
Includes bibliographical references and index.
ISBN 978-1-4777-2823-9 (library binding)—
ISBN 978-1-4777-2825-3 (pbk.)—
SBN 978-1-4777-2826-0 (6-pack)
1. Web site development—Juvenile literature. 2. Web sites—Design—Juvenile literature. I. Title.
TK5105.888.M364 2014
006.7—dc23

2013018137

Manufactured in the United States of America

CPSIA Compliance Information: Batch #W14YA: For further information, contact Rosen Publishing, New York, New York, at 1-800-237-9932.

>>>CONTENTS<<<

We have highlighted blogs, Web sites, and tools throughout this guide in bold; we didn't want to overload you with URLs, but you should be able to find them really easily through search engines.

THE UTTERLY EXCELLENT WORLD OF WEB SITES!

Whether you access it at school or at home, on your computer, games console, or even a mobile phone, the Web plays a huge role in our lives. For most of us, the Web is our first stop when we want to find out more about the world, send emails, play games, communicate with our friends, listen to music, or even check when the next bus is coming. In short, we'd be lost without it.

In this guide, we'll teach you how to get started on building your own Web site. We'll tell you how to make it look great as well as all the lingo from URL to JPEG. We've even thrown in a couple of tricks that mean you won't have to be a super geek to get your Web site online quickly.

Finally, it's worth remembering that Web sites are all about creatively sharing things online that you find interesting. So, as you move through this book, you'll have a chance to start thinking about the ways in which you want to use your Web site. You never know — you might end up being the next Mark Zuckerberg!

GET READY TO DON YOUR CODING CAP AND SUMMON YOUR CREATIVE KARMA FOR THE QUICK EXPERT TEAM'S SHOW-AND-TELL ON:

The man who **invented** the World Wide Web

The woman who became a Web site **millionaire**

How to write code and **create** your very own Web site

All about savvy **teens** who have managed to get **rich** with their Web sites

How to add special **features** to your Web site such as **apps** and widgets

How the **Internet** works and where Web sites live

Chapter 1

GETTING STARTED

✳ WHY BUILD A WEB SITE?

The Web is a great place to find out information, buy things you need, watch videos, and chat with friends. But since you can do all these things in the real world, what makes doing it online so much fun?

Give up?

We think it is because Web sites are all about being creative and making something personal. This means that the Web sites you like to visit tend to look good, be entertaining, and provide an engaging space that allows you to access or share the things that interest you.

These two things — let's call them creativity and individuality — are also what make building your own Web site such a great thing to do. You can make your very own piece of the Web just how you like it and use it to communicate with people who like the same things you do.

✳ WHAT DO I NEED TO GET STARTED ON THE WEB?

The **Web** is part of a global network of connected computers known as the Internet. One of the founding principles of the Web is that it is designed to be accessible to everyone. You don't need to be a computer nerd to build a Web site and it doesn't cost very much to put one online. With a little time and effort you can quickly make a great Web site that will sit right next to those of huge corporations like Amazon or Apple.

also known as the World Wide Web

Even better, you will have your own space to get creative with words, images, and design that will let you tell everyone what you think about the world.

In order to build your first Web site all you will need to get going is:

- **a PC or a Mac**
- **a basic text editor like Notepad on a PC or Simpletext on a Mac**
- **a Web browser such as Internet Explorer or Firefox**

  and

- **your coding hat**

  That's it.

(There is no such thing as a coding hat.
We just like to pretend there is.)

>> TECHIE TALK <<

THE WWW

Most people can't tell the difference, but in reality the Internet and the World Wide Web (WWW) are not the same thing.

The Internet is the name given to a global network of computers that can transfer any kind of digital data (for example email) between them. Whereas the Web is a system of interlinked hypertext documents which can be accessed via the Internet. It is the Web that most of us use to access information, tools, music, and videos.

The Web would not work without three elements: the Uniform Resource Locator, or URL, which helps your computer find a Web page; Hypertext Markup Language, or HTML, which is the publishing language that Web pages are built in; and Hypertext Transfer Protocol, or HTTP, which allows your computer to "talk" to the server on which Web pages are held.

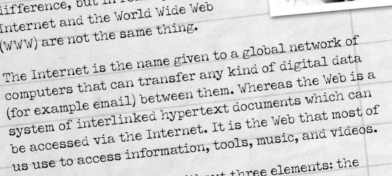

✳ BEFORE YOU BEGIN

Before you type your first line of code, you might like to decide what you want your Web site to be about. Maybe you want to create an online diary or blog all about you and your life, or you want to collect images and videos of your favorite actor, sports team, or band. Perhaps you want to create a Web site to support a project you are working on at school, a sponsored event you are taking part in, or information about a club you belong to. It's your choice.

Once you have decided what kind of content you'd like on your Web site, start to gather everything you will need to fill up its pages. This will save you time later on when you come to build it. Write a draft of the text that you intend to display on the page and think of a name for your Web site such as "My 20 Favorite Hamster Breeds" (don't laugh — we *love* hamsters).

Take some time to compile any images you might like to use. These can be pictures that you've taken, things scanned from magazines, or stuff that you've downloaded online. You should also make a note of the Web addresses of any Web sites you would like to link to.

The best way to keep all these things together is to save them all in one folder somewhere that is easy to find. For example, you could make a folder called "files" for your Web site on your computer's desktop.

stands for information architecture

✳ STRUCTURING A WEB SITE

If you are going have multiple pages on your Web site you will need to think about **IA**. This is a fancy way of saying what pages link to other pages on your Web site. You'll need a **home (or landing) page** that people arrive on first. Then you should create separate pages for different topics that can link off it, for example, a page of photos, information about your Web site, or a page of links you think are interesting. People get bored easily when navigating a Web site, so the IA should be defined by how may clicks it takes to get somewhere. As a rule, the most important information should come first.

page a visitor comes to when they type your Web site address

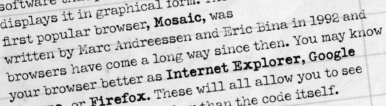

>> TECHIE TALK <<

BROWSERS

A Web browser is a clever piece of software that processes HTML and displays it in graphical form. The first popular browser, **Mosaic,** was written by Marc Andreessen and Eric Bina in 1992 and browsers have come a long way since then. You may know your browser better as **Internet Explorer, Google Chrome,** or **Firefox.** These will all allow you to see what the code means rather than the code itself.

What is really clever about browsers is that they are unbelievably adaptable. You can use just one program to access content, images, email, discussion boards, film, and audio... or even to edit Web sites.

Modern browsers also come with a range of handy plug-ins, or extensions, so you can add games, news, and specialized tools to make them even more useful. Your browser will also tell you if the Web site you are visiting is secure – or safe to use for financial transactions – by displaying a padlock in the address bar.

✴ USABILITY

We all use Web sites differently. Usability is the name given to the study of how easy to read, use, and navigate a Web site is. You should think about usability when you design your pages, as you want your visitors to spend more time viewing your content than trying to work out where everything is.

Here are a couple of key tips for usability that you should try to follow:

- Keep your Web site simple.

- Ensure each page loads fast.

- Put important content near the top so it can be seen without scrolling.

- Lay out pages so visitors can find things easily.

- Make sure menus don't have too many items.

- Ensure your links are descriptive.

✴ CODING YOURSELF VERSUS AN ONLINE SERVICE

When you've thought about structure and gathered together your text and graphics, it's time to think about how you are actually going to build your Web site. You should know that there are two ways by which you can make this happen quickly and easily.

The first is making your own pages, which will mean learning the basics of the coding. The second is using an online service that will host your Web site and let you choose from a range of pre-built templates you can customize to assemble it.

We will show you how to do both of these in this book, but we would recommend that you start by trying to learn a bit of code.

Not only will this give you some real understanding of how the Web works, but it will also stand you in good stead when you want to troubleshoot issues or do more complex and creative things online.

So — without further ado — let's get started with the coding language of the Web, HTML!

Mark Zuckerberg is the computer programmer and entrepreneur behind the social networking site Facebook. He created the site in 2004 while still a student at Harvard University. His top tip:

SAY WHAT?

❝ *All of my friends who have younger siblings who are going to college or high school — my number one piece of advice is: you should learn how to program.* ❞

QUICK EXPERT SUMMARY

- A Web site should be creative and personal.
- Before your start, you should think of a subject for your Web site.
- Collect text, images, and other assets together before you start coding.
- You should plan your Web site's structure to make it easy to use for visitors.
- You can build a Web site by coding it yourself or using an online service.

Chapter 2

ALL ABOUT HTML

✳ WHAT IS HTML?

Web pages are written in HTML. HTML stands for Hypertext Mark-up Language. This is the "hidden" computer code that is used to create Web pages that can be shared with others across the Internet.

HTML is a "mark-up" language, which means that it consists of "tags" that can be read by your browser. They are wrapped around text to create the structure of a page. These tags also tell the browser how to display the text, to add graphics, and to link to other Web sites or interactive elements within a Web page.

✳ Do I have to use HTML?

Yes! Every page that comes through your browser is formatted in HTML. But while HTML tags can be seen by you when you create a Web page and recognized by your browser when it reads it, they will not be visible to the user when he or she visits that page.

HTML is not case sensitive. That means that you can use either lowercase or uppercase when you write it — so <HTML> is the same as <html> to a computer. For consistency, you should use one or the other. It's best not to mix and match.

Your browser will be interested in the version of HTML you are using. Since 1996, the specifications for HTML have been independently maintained by the **World Wide Web Consortium (W3C)**. Each new version of the language is more complex (and more useful) and introduces new tags as well as making old ones obsolete. For example, the current version, HTML 5, allows you to easily create interactive elements that you would have had to build separately before.

>> TECHIE TALK <<

THE CLOUD

You will probably have heard a lot of talk about the cloud. It is a name given to computers and databases that supply computing services across the Internet. The cloud allows people to access these services whenever they like and from anywhere through a browser, a lightweight application, or even a mobile app. Before the cloud, people needed to install programs or store data on their own computers; now they can use someone else's, which can be as big or as small as they like. It is a bit like getting electricity from the power lines rather than using a battery.

The chances are that you are already using the cloud and you don't even know it; for example, **iTunes** holds all the music, films, and apps its users have purchased in the cloud.

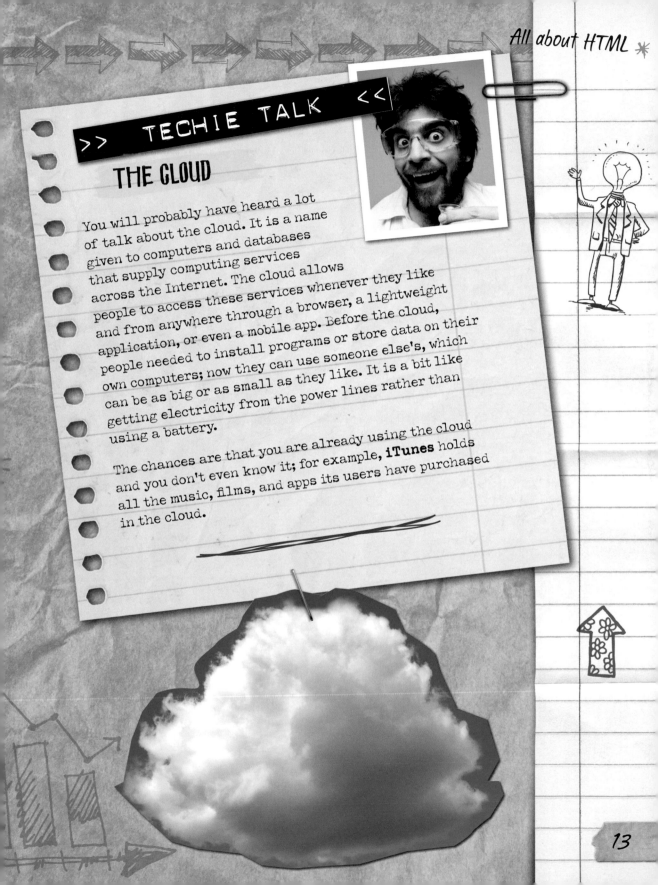

✳ HOW DO YOU WRITE HTML?

The good news is that HTML is easy to learn and follows some fairly simple rules. All you will need to write your first Web page is an eye for detail, a computer, and a bit of practice.

As we have already said, HTML is based around a library of **tags**. These tags consist of text framed by angled brackets: <and>. The angled brackets help the computer distinguish HTML tags from any other text. You'll find these brackets on your keyboard just above the comma and the full stop.

The written instructions to the browser found between these brackets are called **elements**. While these elements look like some kind of complex code, in fact at first they are almost always basic abbreviations of the tag's purpose.

For example, the tag <hr> tells your browser to create a horizontal rule.

A tag may also have **attributes**. This is additional information about how to use the tag.

For example, height=45 tells the browser to display the image referred to in a tag with a height of 45 pixels.

SAY WHAT?

" When I took office [as President], only high energy physicists had ever heard of what is called the World Wide Web.... Now even my cat has its own page. "

Bill Clinton, US President from 1993 to 2001

REALITY CHECK

☑ **Online critters**

Michael Acton Smith is best known as the online genius behind Moshi Monsters. In his early twenties, he co-founded an online gadget and gift retailer called **Firebox.com** with his university friend Tom Boardman. They started the business with a $1,600 loan from Michael's mother and free use of an old attic space. Within five years, it was one of the fastest-growing private businesses in the UK.

Most people would have been pretty happy with this success, but Michael's dream was to build the biggest entertainment brand in the world for a new digital generation of kids. So, in 2004, he launched the online games developer **Mind Candy**. Its first product was an ambitious global treasure hunt game called Perplex City, but this was soon swept away by the phenomenal success of Moshi Monsters.

Moshi Monsters allows children aged 6–10 to collect and look after friendly looking monsters online, as well as solve puzzles, read stories, play games, and chat with friends. It now has 65 million users around the world and has expanded into the offline world of toys, magazines, books, and trading cards. With new creatures being added every day and the brand still growing, Michael's company is now valued at $200 million.

OFFICIAL FORM C-185A

✷ TYPES OF HTML TAG

In an ideal world, HTML would be entirely regular, but, like any language, it is constantly changing and evolving, so you will find a few oddities. For instance, there are two kinds of HTML tags: **container tags** and **empty tags**.

A **container tag** wraps around text or graphics and always comes in a set that includes a matched opening and closing tag. For example:

<html> is an opening tag.
</html> is a closing tag.

Everything after the opening tag will be affected by the element, while the forward slash (/) in the closing tag tells the browser that the instruction has ended.

However, **empty tags** stand alone. For example, the tag <br>, or break, tells the browser to add a line break. Empty tags do not have to be wrapped around **copy** and do not require a closing tag.

The good news is that there are only a handful of empty tags, so, as a general rule, assume that every tag you open will need to be closed.

another word for text that is published in print or online

GET REAL! A Web site as the perfect platform for your thoughts

Louis (13) runs a journalistic Web site: "My Web site allows me to tell the world what I think and what I'm doing. It also allows my readers to tell me what they think. I want to start using video and sound, too."

Viewing the source code of a page can help you to see how it was made and is probably one of the best ways to learn how HTML works. One of the great things about your trusty browser is that it will let you peek at the HTML code that was used to create any Web page you visit. Here's how you do it:

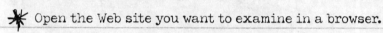

* Open the Web site you want to examine in a browser.

* Right click anywhere in the page (or hold down the control key and click if you have a Mac).

* Click on "View Page Source" in the page menu.

* Now you can see the code of that page.

* Try using your browser to look at some HTML code. At first glance, this will probably look pretty complex, but keep doing it as you move through this book. As you learn more about HTML, you will recognize pieces of code and get a better sense of what they do on the page. In fact, if you see something you like, you could even cut and paste the code to use on your own Web page.

QUICK EXPERT SUMMARY

* The language of the Internet is HTML.

* HTML is a coding language in which tags are wrapped around content.

* HTML tags contain elements and attributes describing their purpose.

* You can see the code used to create any Web page by using your browser.

* You can use both container and empty tags.

Chapter 3

BUILDING A WEB PAGE

✱ MAKING YOUR FIRST WEB PAGE

Okay, so we've got a handle on the basics of HTML. Now it's time to switch on the computer and begin to look at the structure of an HTML page.

All HTML pages are divided into two main parts: the **head** and the **body**. The head contains information about the page and the body holds the content that is displayed to a Web site's visitors.

So far, so good. To create your first page, you will need four primary tags: <html>, <head>, <title>, and <body>. These are all container tags, so remember that they must have a beginning and an end.

<html> </html>

Every HTML page begins and ends with the <html> tag. This tells the browser that the document is an HTML file.

<head> </head>

The <head> tag contains general information about the page, such as keywords for search engines or a description.

<title> </title>

The <title> tag appears within the <head> tag and tells the browser the title of the page, for example "My 20 Favorite Hamster Breeds."

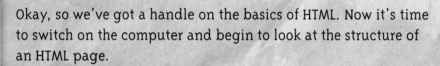

`<body> </body>`

The main content of your page is placed within the body tags, for example text, images, links, tables, and graphics.

So a simple HTML page would look like this:

`<html>`

`<head>`

`<title>My 20 Favorite Hamster Breeds</title>`

`</head>`

`<body>`

Welcome to my hamster homepage!

`</body>`

`</html>`

It really is that simple.

You don't have to space your tags out as we have done (because the computer won't care), but it helps to do so as it will make them easier for you to read.

✳ Nesting

As the number of tags on your page grows, you will need to find a way to navigate them. The best way to do this is to lay out your Web page using a structure called **Nesting**. This means that each new set of tags is placed inside other tags like the layers of an onion.

On our page, the <title> tags are nested inside the <head> tags, while <head> and <body> tags are nested inside the <html> tags. Remember that you will have to close all the container tags that you have opened, so nesting is essential if you want to keep track of them.

Okay, it's the moment of truth. Let's create and save your first HTML document!

Open your text editor and key in the simple HTML code laid out on the previous page.

When you are finished, open the "file" menu and using the "save as" function, save your file somewhere easy to find, for instance your desktop. You can name the file whatever you like, but the first page in a Web site is usually called index or default. It is very important that you add ".html" to the end of the file name, so the browser knows that it is a Web page, for example "index.html."

To view your page, either double-click on it to open it up in your browser OR open your browser, go to the browser's "File" menu, select "Open file," and navigate to your page.

Hey presto! You've made your first Web page.

Dude!

✳ FORMATTING TEXT

Congratulations — you now have your first HTML page! Some of you may have noticed that to add text to your page, you simply type whatever you like between the <body> tags. But hold your horses, because you can use other tags to make this text easier to read and a lot more interesting to look at.

✳ Titles and headings

You can create titles in your page by using the **heading tag**. This is represented in HTML as — you guessed it — <h>. There are six levels of heading tag ranging from <h1> to <h6>. These tags will change the size of your text from big <h1> to small <h6> and render it in bold.

Behind the scenes, heading tags will also serve a vital purpose by telling search engines such as **Google** what the most important information on your page is, based on the heading tags you have used. So it is important that your tags run in order with the most important thing — the title of the page — first.

For example:

`<h1> My 20 Favorite Hamster Breeds </h1>`

✳ Spacing and formatting

To create paragraphs and add space between them, you use the **paragraph tag**. Guess what? This is represented in HTML as `<p>`. This is a container tag and wraps around the text that makes up each individual paragraph.

For example:

`<p>Hello. I have decided to build a Web page to tell people all about the most amazing hamster breeds in the world.</p>`

To add a single line of space, you can use the **break tag** represented as `<br>`. This is an empty tag and stands alone, so you won't need to wrap it.

For example:

`<p>The Siberian hamster is my absolute favorite, and here's why:<br>`

`It's also called the Russian winter dwarf hamster.<br>`

`Its fur changes color in the winter.<br>`

`It has a racing stripe on its back.`

`</p>`

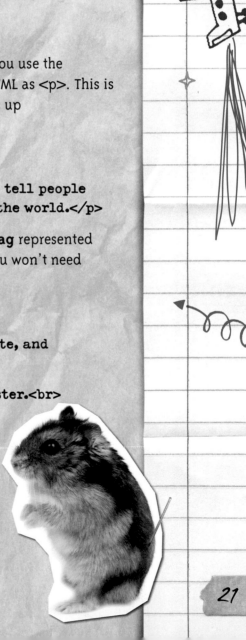

✳ Splitting a section

To divide content on your page into sections, there is a quick and easy way to create a dividing line. You simply use the **horizontal rule tag**, or <hr>. Like the break tag, this is also an empty tag.

✳ Adding emphasis to words and phrases

You may also want to add emphasis to words in the text using bold or italics. To create bold text use: .... To create italicized text use: <i>...</i>. However, use both these effects sparingly or they will lose their impact. Be particularly careful with the <i>, as italics can sometimes be difficult to read on screen.

✳ ADDING LISTS

You may have a lot to say, but you need to be careful that your page is easy to read online. Nothing but blocks of dense text will make it hard going for readers, so an easy way to present content that falls together under a single topic is in a list. Lists in HTML can be presented as both numbered or **ordered lists** and bulleted or **unordered lists.**

Lists are nested. If you remember what we said about onions, this means that there is a pair of nested tags that identify the type of list, and then within that tag there are other tags that itemize each element or **list item**. For example:

<ol> </ol>

The ordered list is a container tag and is used for numbered lists.

<ul> </ul>

The unordered list is a container tag and is used for bulleted lists.

`<li> </li>`

The list item tag is a container tag and is nested within the ordered or unordered tags.

You can see the difference between the two list styles below.

An ordered (numbered) list is coded like this:

`<ol>`

`<li>It's also called the Russian winter dwarf hamster.</li>`

`<li>Its fur changes color in the winter.</li>`

`<li>It has a racing stripe on its back.</li>`

`</ol>`

In the browser, it will look like this:

1. It's also called the Russian winter dwarf hamster.

2. Its fur changes color in the winter.

3. It has a racing stripe on its back.

An unordered (bulleted) list is coded like this:

`<ul>`

`<li>It's also called the Russian winter dwarf hamster.</li>`

`<li>Its fur changes color in the winter.</li>`

`<li>It has a racing stripe on its back.</li>`

`</ul>`

In the browser, it will look like this:

- It's also called the Russian winter dwarf hamster.

- Its fur changes color in the winter.

- It has a racing stripe on its back.

DIY DUDE

Update your HTML page

It's now time to update your HTML pages using some of the new code we've learned. You might also start adding your own content. You could use the text suggested while you are learning, or start adding your own text as ours is – well – a little "specialist," shall we say.

Open up your HTML file in your text editor and type in the additional text (or your text) and code that we've looked at using paragraph and list tags.

When you have finished, save the page by using the "save" function in the "file" menu. You could use a keyboard shortcut instead. Try hitting the S key while holding down the CTRL button. It will also save the page and might save you a bit of time. Use the Apple button instead of CTRL if you've got a Mac.

Dude!

Now return to your browser. Nothing has happened!

Don't panic. All you need to do is refresh the page to see the changes you have made. You can find the "refresh" or "reload" option under the "view" menu. Alternatively, use a keyboard shortcut again; in this case, hit the "F5" key on your keyboard while holding down the CTRL button. Again, you can use the Apple button instead of CTRL if you've got a Mac. Your changes should now appear.

By amending your HTML file and refreshing the browser as you go, you will be able to browse changes as you make them to slowly build up your page.

✳ ADDING IMAGES

They say a picture paints a thousand words... which is a fancy way to explain that images really help to make a page come alive, so you'll definitely want some. Whether it is a photograph, cartoon, or logo, remember that any picture is adding something to the content on your page so try to get them to illustrate what you are saying in words.

Images can be imported to your computer using a scanner or downloaded from a digital camera. It's also really easy to browse and download the millions of images that can be found online. To find images online, simply go to the **Google** Web site and click the "images" tab on the page. Now you can search and browse images from all over the Web. If you find one you like, simply right click (or, if you are using a Mac, hold the control key and click) and hit "save picture as" to download it to your computer.

✳ USING IMAGES AND COPYRIGHT

Before you go foraging for images, a quick word of warning. While it is easy to find pictures for every occasion online, be aware that, technically, using other people's images could be an infringement of copyright (which means unauthorized usage, and is against the law).

In practice, you're allowed "fair use" of images, which means that if they are given proper attribution and used for a personal Web site, there shouldn't be a problem. For example, if you are commenting on a picture or using it for research, and not merely reproducing it, you won't usually be infringing copyright.

25

REALITY CHECK

☑ Martha Lane Fox

Martha Lane Fox was one of the first stars of the Internet. She was the co-founder of the Web site **Lastminute.com,** which offered deals on flights, gifts, and hotel rooms. Selling shares in the company made her a millionaire when she was just 27 years old.

In recent years, she has been better known as the UK's Digital Champion and spearheads the government's efforts to get everyone online via the **Go ON UK** campaign.

Martha is dedicated to helping everyone be more tech savvy because she believes it is an important part of living and working in the modern world. She says: "I don't think you can be a proper citizen of our society in the future if you are not engaged online."

OFFICIAL FORM C-185A

A good way around this issue is to use images that are explicitly approved for use by others. There are banks of images, such as **Morguefile**, where you are free to use most images without worrying about copyright, provided that your site is not for commercial gain. You can also search using the **Creative Commons** Web site, which draws on various image banks. You will usually need to give credit on your Web site if you use a picture that you've found in this way, but you can find more details on their Help pages.

✳ IMAGE FORMATS

Images can use a lot of computer memory, so big images will make your page load slowly. You will need to create and size your images and photographs using graphics software. If you want to make really professional looking images, you might like to look at **Adobe Photoshop** or **Paintshop Pro** (a shareware program). However, a free opensource alternative is the **GNU Image Manipulation Program** which can be downloaded at **gimp.org**.

Special file formats for images are used on the Internet to help reduce the amount of memory they use while still looking good. These are **GIF** (Graphic Interchange Format) files, **JPEG** (Joint Photographic Experts Group) files, and **PNG** (Portable Network Graphic) files.

As a general rule, **GIFs** are good for simple images, such as logos, and **JPEGs** are good for photographs. PNGs are pretty good at everything.

pronounced "jay-peg"

pronounced "ping"

✳ THE IMAGE TAG

To place an image onto your Web page, you will need to use the **image tag** <img>. There are two very important things to remember about the image tag. It's an empty tag, so there's no closing tag, but it will require **attributes** to be effective. If you remember, an attribute is the word code used to describe extra data for the browser about a tag's function, for example the size of an image.

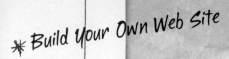

The code for adding an image tag looks like this:

src – identifies the image's name and tells the browser where to get it

height and width – tells the browser the size of the image in pixels

<img src="files/siberianhamster.jpg" width="149" height="140" alt="Picture of a Siberian hamster in the meadows of Mongolia">

alt – gives alternative text to describe the image. This is read by search engines such as Google and used by assistive software such as screen readers used by blind people

Hamster?

Meadows of Mongolia

>> TECHIE TALK <<

MULTIMEDIA

Multimedia is simply a way to describe when different media such as images, text, film, and music are mixed together. The Web is very much a multimedia environment in which different media can be drawn into a Web page or linked to create an interactive experience for the user.

When designing your pages, you might like to think about how you can use film and sound to make your pages more interesting, and to describe what you are talking about by using different types of media.

For example, you might think a particular singer or band is great, so why not put one of their videos on your page so everyone else can see them in action. Though as we have already said, unless you've made it yourself, you will need to be careful to ensure that you have permission to use any material that you post on the Web.

✳ ADDING LINKS

The Web is all about **hyperlinks**. It's these links that allow Web users to jump from one site to another. You can use links to show people Web sites you like on the Web. Without links, we might as well stick with printed books!

Most important for us, links are also how you can get users to move between pages on your Web site. We've seen how to build a single Web page, but to create a Web site you will need to make some more pages and make some links to connect them together.

There are two things you need to create a link:

👁 the name of a file or the URL you want to link to;

👁 the link **hotspot** which is the highlighted text or graphic that can be clicked on to get to where you want to go.

To create a link in HTML, you will need the **anchor (or link) tag <a>**. This is a container tag, so it will wrap around the text or image you want to make into a link like this:

<a> </a>

stands for hypertext reference

Inside the tag, you need an **HREF** attribute to tell the browser where to go. So the **basic code for a link looks like this:**

a – this stands for "anchor" and that tells the browser this is a link

href – the hypertext reference tells the browser where to go on the Internet

**<a href="http//:www.kingofhamsters.co.uk">
The ultimate hamster breed Web site </a>**

url – this is the destination of the link

text – this is the text that will be linked to the destination of the Web page

✳ USEFUL HTML TAGS

Below is a list of some of the most commonly used HTML tags.

<a> Short for anchor; tells the browser a link is to follow

<body> The body content of the document, or everything you see on screen

  Creates a single line break in the text

<center> Moves text to the center

<h1> to <h6> Used to size and order headings

<head> Information about a page

<hr> Short for horizontal line; draws a line across the page

<i> Creates italic text

<img> Short for image; tells the browser an image is to follow

<li> Creates a list; used with <ol> or <ul>

<ol> Short for ordered list; creates a numbered list

<p> Creates a paragraph

<strong> Creates bold text

<table> Tells the browser to create a data table

<td> A data cell in a table

<title> Title for a page

<tr> A row in a table

<ul> Short for unordered list; creates a bullet point list

There are too many HTML tags to list here, but you can find a great quick reference document for all of them at **htmlgoodies.com**.

DIY DUDE

Adding some links

Dude!

To make another Web page, quickly run through the page creation process we have already covered. Don't forget that you'll need some different text and images on your new page and you'll need to call it something unique. When you name your new page, you should follow some simple rules:

* Don't leave spaces in the file name.

* Always end with either ".html" or ".htm" to tell a browser that this is a Web page.

* Don't use funny symbols, such as \$, %, ^, &.

Choose the "save as" option on the "file" menu and name your page, for example "photos.html."

Now return to your original page and type in your link code, but reference your new page as part of the resource location in the URL. So:

<a href="http://www.kingofhamsters.co.uk/photos. html"> Follow this link to see some pictures of hamsters from around the world </a>

Save the page and refresh your browser. You should now see your highlighted link. Click it and the browser will take you to your new page.

You just made your first link and your first Web site at the same time!

>> TECHIE TALK <<

MORE URLS

If you are an eagle-eyed Web user, you can use the bit at the end of an address in the URL (the suffix) to give you some additional information about the purpose and location of the Web site you are visiting. While this is all useful detective work, do bear in mind that these names are only guidelines as people can actually purchase any name.

Here are commonly used organizational suffixes:

.com – US based business

.edu – US based university

.gov – US based government organization

.org – US based charity or voluntary organisation

.net – networked service provider

.info – site with general information

There are also many commonly used national suffixes, for example:

.uk – United Kingdom

.fr – France

.es – Spain

.de – Germany

.it – Italy

.eu – European Union

.com – USA

.in – India

.cn – China

.jp – Japan

.au – Australia

✳ ADDING A TABLE

Tables were originally used to display data, but HTML developers soon realized that they could also be a quick and easy way to present elements on a Web page. A table is divided into rows (signified by the <tr> tag), and each row is divided into data cells (using the <td> tag). A <td> (or table data) tag can contain text, links, images, or even other tables, and lock them into place using this grid.

Writing a table is quite simple, but it can be a bit tedious and involves a fair bit of typing. For example:

```
<table border = "1">

<tr>

<td>Hamster breeds</td>

<td>Hamster habitats</td>

</tr>

<tr>

<td>My personal favorites</td>

<td>Top pet hamster breeds</td>

</tr>

</table>
```

The table should look like this:

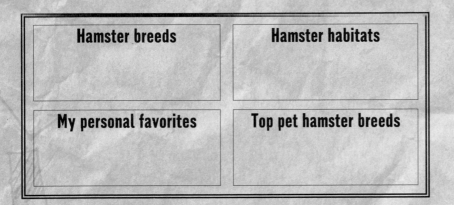

| Hamster breeds | Hamster habitats |
| My personal favorites | Top pet hamster breeds |

When you display the results in your browser, you will see the grid of the table around the content. This is useful when you are first creating a table, but you can get rid of it when you are finished by setting the border attribute to "0": <table border = "0">.

✳ HTML EDITORS

As we have already seen, any basic text editor like **Notepad** on a PC or **TextEdit** on a Mac can be used to build a Web page, but there are a whole range of HTML editors that will help you do the job even better.

An HTML editor is a program that will help you format and browse your code. You may want to get hold of a basic source code editor such as **BBEdit** or one of the more complicated editors such as **Adobe Dreamweaver** or **Microsoft Publisher**. Most of these will lay out your code in different colors so you can see individual types of tags and separate them from the copy easily.

http://www.barebones.com

what you see is what you get

Many hold code libraries so you don't have to remember all those nit-picky tags. Some will even allow you to drag and drop text and images to create your site as it looks in a browser, using a **WYSIWYG** mode.

In fact, if you really want to cheat, even word processing programs such as **Microsoft Word** will allow you to save a document as HTML and do all the coding for you, so you won't need to know any HTML at all. However it is best to avoid using Word in this way when you are starting out. While it may help you build a Web page quickly, just as with online services you won't learn anything about HTML. Besides, if the code doesn't do what you expect it to, you will really struggle to fix it.

QUICK EXPERT SUMMARY

- There are two main parts to an HTML page – the head and body.

- HTML tags are nested in the code.

- You can write HTML in a simple text editor and view it in any browser.

- You can format text in HTML as well as adding images, lists, and links to other Web sites.

- Lists are a great way to break up content.

- Images can be JPEGs, GIFs, or PNGs.

- Be aware of copyright when sourcing images.

DESIGNING YOUR WEB SITE

✳ MAKING IT LOOK GOOD

So we have seen how HTML can be used to define the words, images, and links on a Web page, but you will still need to tell the browser how you would like your Web pages to look. This is your chance to add loads of creativity and color to help make your page stand out. This is done with the help of a coding language called CSS, by which you can create a style sheet.

Styling allows you to add information to a page that can be read by your browser. It defines the design of your Web site and how each page is displayed. Your choice of style might define the background of your page, the color of any links, and what font the text should be displayed in, for example.

You can do this in one of two ways:

 **You can put a separate style sheet on each page.**
Or
 **You can create one style sheet and link all your pages to it.**

We only have so much time in this book, so we will just look at adding some styling to an individual page. However, there are loads of great styling resources online. We recommend a visit to **CSS Zen Garden** at **ccszengarden.com** to see some fantastic examples of what styling your page can do. Designers use CSS to make their Web sites look radically different, and CSS Zen Garden shows how much Web sites can stand out with good styling.

✳ DEFINING COLORING AND SIZE

Color and text size can be defined in two ways in style sheets — one easy and the other a bit trickier.

A color can be defined by its name, such as "orange," or by a more precise hexadecimal definition. A hexadecimal color is a six-digit number used to represent the red, green, and blue components of that color. The first two digits are red, the second two digits are green, and the third two are blue. The colors run from 0 to 6, then A to F. Numbers mean low and letters mean high amounts of that color. So, the "hex color" for white is #ffffff and the "hex color" for black is #000000.

Likewise, size can be defined by a simple number from 1 to 5, with 1 being the largest, or a more precise definition in points, for example 12pt.

>> TECHIE TALK <<

CSS

CSS (Cascading Style Sheets) is a style sheet language used to define the presentation of pages written in a mark-up language such as HTML.

CSS allows the separation of the page's content from its presentation. This enables multiple pages to share the same formatting, reducing the repetition of code, and allowing the same page to be presented in different ways, for example on a computer screen or in a printable version.

Where there are multiple design instructions in a page, the CSS will specify which one is used first and where it applies if it is used more than once in a page. This is called a cascade; hence the name. CSS specifications are maintained by the **World Wide Web Consortium,** or W3C for short.

http://www.w3.org

✳ WRITING A STYLE SHEET

Style sheets may seem tricky when you first look at them, but similar to HTML they also use attributes to tell the browser what to do. CSS syntax consists of only three parts and they are always written like this:

selector { property: value }

Don't worry, this is easier than it looks. Here's what that means:

- **selector** — the HTML element that you want to style (such as a heading tag).

- **property** — the aspect of the element you want to style (such as the font in which the element is displayed).

- **value** — defines how the style is applied (such as displaying a font in red).

You will need to remember that HTML attributes are usually framed by angle brackets, like **<attribute>**, whereas style sheets hold their attributes with curly brackets (they really are called that!) or braces, like this: **{attribute}**.

❝ *Imagine a world in which every single person on the planet is given free access to the sum of all human knowledge. That's what we're doing.* ❞

Jimmy Wales, founder of Wikipedia

SAY WHAT?

✳ ADDING A STYLE SHEET TO YOUR PAGE

Let's see how this might work if we add a style sheet to our page. To do this, you will need to follow a few rules:

◉ It must be within the <head> and </head> commands.

◉ The text must be surrounded by <style type="text/css"> and </style>

◉ The style sheet is text, so if you just type it on the page, it will be visible in the browser. In addition to the style commands above, surround the text with <!-- and -->. Those commands are known as **comments** and will stop the browser from displaying the text.

When you're all done, the format will look like this:

```
<head>
<style type="text/css">
<!--

Style sheet information goes in here...

-->
</style>
</head>
```

Let's look at an actual example of CSS in action:

```
<html>

<head>

<style type="text/css">

<!--

body

{

background-color:#d0e4fe;

}
```

See blue bullet point on right

```
h1
```
See pink bullet point below
```
{
color:red;
text-align:center;
font-family:"verdana";
}
p
```
See green bullet point below
```
{
font-family:"arial";
font-size:20px;
}
-->
</style>
<title>My top-twenty hamster breeds</title>
</head>
```

- **background-color** — tells the browser what color to make the page.

- **h₁** — tells the browser which font and color to use for the heading.

- **p** — tells the browser which font and color to use for the text within paragraph tags.

DIY DUDE

Adding some CSS

You can probably imagine what's coming next... That's right – you are going to add some styling to your Web page. Open a new document in your text editor and type in the code on the previous page. You can change the colors and fonts to whatever you like.

When you are done, save the file and reload the page.

✱ **Is your page starting to look beautiful yet?**

Dude!

SOME DESIGN DOS AND DON'TS

Whether you build it yourself or are amending a template, here are some tips that might help as you decide on the look of your pages...

- DO choose a color scheme and design that suits you and the theme of your Web site.

- DO try making some images of your own so your page is totally unique.

- DO make sure that the fonts and color schemes you use aren't difficult to look at, so DON'T use dark fonts on a dark background or bright, neon colors.

- DO use a larger font for titles (h1 or h2).

- DON'T be afraid to leave white space on your page. A cluttered Web page is hard to read. Less can be more in Web design.

- DON'T use too many widgets and large images, as they can slow the time it takes to load a page.

Of course, it's up to you to decide what to feature and how to present it, so don't be afraid to experiment!

42

GET REAL! Web site design

Rosa (14) enjoys creating and sharing images on her Web site: "I like designing things and editing photos, and publishing them on my Web site allows me to do this easily. I like that my Web site is individual and is something I can show my friends."

QUICK EXPERT SUMMARY

- Style sheets define the look and feel of a page.

- A style sheet can be added to each page or one style sheet can be applied to many pages.

- Style sheets are made up of a selector, a property, and a value.

- Where HTML uses <and> to define an element, style sheets use {and}.

- Ensure you leave white space on your pages and avoid color schemes that make it hard to read.

GETTING YOUR STUFF ONLINE QUICKLY

* USING AN ONLINE SERVICE

We have looked at the basics of HTML coding and how to add design elements to a page, but if you are pressed for time (or want to cheat) you could build a Web site even faster by using templates made by someone else and tweaking them.

There are lots of online services that will help you do this. Usually they will provide a free service for a limited number of pages, but you may need to pay a small fee if you want your own domain name or if you want to create a big Web site with a lot of pictures and videos.

* How does it work?

All you need to do is a bit of basic planning before you start. You will need to think about the IA of the Web site you want to build. You will also need to decide what images and content you want to use. You could take a look at some of the sample sites on the service's Web site, find one that's similar to what you want, and, without stealing too many ideas, make something like it.

These are a few of the services you might want to look at:

- ⓖ **Webs.com** — will let you create a number of pages designed to carry content, photos, and video with your choice of templates. **Webs.com**

- ⓖ **Squidoo** — can be a quick and easy solution for making a single page. **squidoo.com**

- ⓖ **Weebly** — lets you create a site and a blog, but you will need your own domain name or to pay to register one of theirs. **weebly.com**

- ⓖ **Yola** — offers professional-looking Web sites with your own domain name. **yola.com**

- ⓖ **Moonfruit** — offers drag and drop based Web site creation with the ability to upgrade for more options. **moonfruit.com**

Steve Jobs was the founder and CEO of Apple Inc. He was a leading figure in the growth of personal computing and has been described as the "father of the digital revolution." Jobs believed in the ideas of the young generation:

SAY WHAT?

❝ Older people sit down and ask, 'What is it?' but the boy asks, 'What can I do with it?'. ❞

✳ BUILDING A SITE WITH WEBS.COM

It seems too good to be true, but it really does only take a few minutes to create a Web site with one of these online services. Let's look at the process with one of the biggest — **Webs.com**.

1 ◎ As before, save any copy, graphics, or films you want to use in a place where you can find them before you start.

2 ◎ Go to Webs.com and hit "start now."

3 ◎ Create an account by entering some basic details such as an email address to contact you, your choice of password, and the address you want for your site — for example, "tophamsters." This will create the URL tophamsters.Webs.com.

4 ◎ Choose a background template.

5 ◎ Select a home page.

6 ◎ Drag and drop the page elements you want to display on your home page; for example, headings, text areas, and images. You will need to click into these elements in the site builder tool to add content or multimedia.

7 ◎ Use the tool bar which appears on the page to format text and add links.

8 ◎ Add additional pages by selecting them from the template bar at the foot of the page. You will need to add content and links to these pages using the same drag and drop process.

9 ◎ Choose "publish" and your basic site should be published straight away.

You can update your site at any time. Don't forget to add a link to your site at the bottom of your emails and tell people about it — nobody's going to visit a Web site they don't know about.

REALITY CHECK

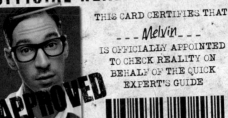

OFFICIAL REALITY CHECKER

THIS CARD CERTIFIES THAT

_ _ _ _Melvin_ _ _

IS OFFICIALLY APPOINTED
TO CHECK REALITY ON
BEHALF OF THE QUICK
EXPERT'S GUIDE

APPROVED

Three teen Internet success stories

☑ Jamal Edwards – SBTV

Jamal Edwards started his media empire as a teenager running around his west London neighborhood filming local bands on his handycam and putting the results on **YouTube**. This soon evolved into the Web site **SBTV**, a youth lifestyle broadcaster with a ten-strong production team that provides a unique take on the latest news, sports, fashion, and music releases. The SBTV brand now has over 50 million YouTube views and tens of thousands of **Facebook** subscribers and continues to grow year after year. sb-tv.co.uk

☑ Pete Cashmore – Mashable

Pete Cashmore is the CEO and founder of the blog **Mashable.com**, which publishes the latest developments in social media, mobile, and gadgets. He started Mashable in his house when he was 19 years old. The site now enjoys some 50 million page views a month. Pete has become a Web-celebrity as well as amassing an estimated fortune of US$70 million. mashable.com

☑ Catherine Cook – MeetMe

Catherine Cook created the Web site **MyYearBook.com** in 2005 (now called **meetme.com**) when she was still a teenager. The site mixes elements of **Facebook** and **Friends Reunited** to create a social network aimed at those under 18. Despite starting small, Catherine has made an estimated $30 million fortune through revenue raised from advertising on the Web site. meetme.com

OFFICIAL FORM C-185A

✷ ADDING WIDGETS AND APPS

When you are using an online service such as **Webs.com**, there are usually a host of free widgets you can add to your page. "Widget" is the name given to small pieces of reusable code that can be added to your Web site.

Usually they are used to add live information, like a scrolling news feed; search tools for useful things like looking up train times; interactive elements like a small game; or maybe to draw in video and audio that is hosted elsewhere. You could even add a form to help your friends get in touch with you.

In short, widgets will add professional-looking functionality to your page that you'd have to be a programming whizz to create from scratch.

In the same tool bar that you use to create new pages, you will find the option to add widgets to your page. Simply drag, drop, and publish, and you are on your way!

Don't forget that you will need to configure them a little bit to do what you want. For example, if you add a video widget, you will still need to tell it where to find the video you want to play, such as its location on YouTube.

You might also like to add a widget from another Web site. In most cases, this will be given as a few lines of code. But don't worry if it looks a bit complex, you just need to paste the whole thing in. The widget will show on your Web site, but its code will draw in any graphics, functionality, and data that it needs from the host's Web site.

>> TECHIE TALK <<

OPEN SOURCE SOFTWARE

Open source software is the name given to products that can be accessed for free online. Behind it is a new philosophy of digital development in which unpaid programmers work together over the Internet to develop software that is made available for all to use with no charge.

Open source software has been developed for lots of different purposes – server operating systems such as **LINUX**, word processing such as **Open Office**, graphics such as **GIMP**, and blogs and Web sites such as **Wordpress** and **Drupal**.

http://www.gimp.org

✳ CHANGING AND UPDATING TEMPLATES

Even though it is embarrassingly easy to build a Web site with a free service, you will still want to make it personal to you. Try experimenting with different templates and features until you find a design that you're happy with.

Most of these sites will offer a selection of templates and themes that you can choose from. However, they will also allow you to change font colors and even the background images. You will find that the basic knowledge of Web design you have already picked up will really help you to personalize your Web site.

DIY DUDE

Add a video widget

Dude!

Let's try to use the video widget on a Webs.com Web site in four simple steps:

1. Find a video you would like to use. This might be one you have on your computer or one hosted on a video sharing Web site such as YouTube.

2. Insert the video into your page by clicking on the video button in the widget bar at the foot of the page in "builder mode" and simply drag the video to wherever you want.

3. You will be prompted to upload the video from your computer, link to it on YouTube, or paste in the hyperlink reference to the video from another Web site.

4. Click the "insert video" button.

That's it, your done! If you want to change your video, simply double-click on it and repeat the process.

QUICK EXPERT SUMMARY

- There are many free services that will let you create a Web site online.
- These services offer pre-made templates that you can configure.
- You will need to have a good idea of what you want your Web site to be before you start.
- Keep your design simple and don't use too many colors.
- Widgets are small pieces of code that can be added to your Web site.

THE INTERNET'S NUTS AND BOLTS

So you have now built your first very own Web site. And it's looking great. Before you go forth into the world of programming and create your Internet emporium, we think it's worth knowing a thing or two about the Web — how it all started, how it works, and what "Internet" actually means.

✳ WHERE DID THE INTERNET COME FROM?

You may find it hard to imagine a time when there wasn't an Internet, but it is a relatively recent invention.

The idea for the Internet was born when techies working for the US Advanced Research Projects Agency (ARPA) were asked by the United States Department of Defense to design a method to ensure communications in time of war between the military and research facilities. In 1969, they succeeded by connecting together computers at the University of California and the Stanford Research Institute. This baby Internet was known as ARPANET.

Similar networks were also being developed in other countries, but the really clever thing about ARPANET was that it used a system called TCP/IP. This allowed the network to pass high volume "packets" of information. It is still in use today.

✷ The modern Internet

By 1971, 40 more networks had been connected to ARPANET.

The name "**Internet**" was coined to describe these new connected networks. It's not a very imaginative name, but it does the job.

"inter" means between, and "net" is short for network

You would not recognize the early Internet. It was entirely text-based and about one-third of its traffic was basic email. The World Wide Web as we know it was not created until 1989 with the invention of "hypertext." Hypertext allowed users to browse between documents across the Internet using hyperlinks and to format them in a universal, easy-to-read way.

The first Web page was published in 1991, and, as this new code was made available to all, it opened the Internet up to everyone. It made Web sites cheap and easy to build so you didn't have to be wearing a lab coat to make one. Today, there are over half a billion active Web sites on the Web, with millions more being added every month.

http://

What's more, you can now connect to the Web from almost anywhere in the world and beyond! The first live Internet link from low earth orbit was established in 2010 when T. J. Creamer, an astronaut on the International Space Station, posted an update to his **Twitter** account using the space station's high-speed Ku band microwave link.

REALITY CHECK

☑ Tim Berners-Lee

Tim Berners-Lee is a computer scientist who is considered to be the father of the modern Internet by developing the World Wide Web. While working at a particle physics lab in the 1990s, he became frustrated that he could not share information easily with his fellow researchers. While the scientists did have a shared computer network, everyone worked on their own bit of it. His solution was to develop a system that would allow users of the network to create links between documents called **hyperlinks** so they could reference and jump to other related information easily. He called this enhanced form of document "hypertext."

Since the creation of the Web, Tim Berners-Lee has continued to be closely involved in its development. He is also the founder of The World Wide Web Consortium (W3C), which sets the coding standards and good practice guidelines for the Internet today.

Despite the huge global impact of his invention, Tim Berners-Lee remains a true techie and insists he was simply putting together existing ideas. "I just had to take the hypertext idea and connect it to the Transmission Control Protocol and domain name system ideas and – ta-da! – the World Wide Web."

He makes it sound so easy, anyone could do it!

OFFICIAL FORM C-185A

✳ WHERE DO WEB SITES LIVE?

All Web sites need to live somewhere — this is called **hosting**. Your Web host is a dedicated computer known as a **server** which sits in a building somewhere in the world. This is where your Web site is actually kept when you put it on the Internet.

As we have already seen, the Internet is a global network of connected computers, so it doesn't matter where you live or where your server is located — you could be in London, but your Web site could be hosted in New York, Paris, Mumbai, or even in the Amazon jungle!

As we have already mentioned, the bad news is that even if you build your own Web site, Web hosting is something for which you might have to pay. Don't worry, it won't be much, but you will need someone with a credit card to pay for it.

Choosing a Web hosting provider is easy. There are a huge number of Web hosts out there and most offer a similar service for a small charge. Try to do your some research with someone who has done it before and keep an eye out for free options closer to home before you fork out your own cash — for example, your school or a friend might have some space you could borrow.

Of course, while you are building your Web site you don't need to buy any hosting. It's only once you're happy with it that you need to think about how you'd like to get it online.

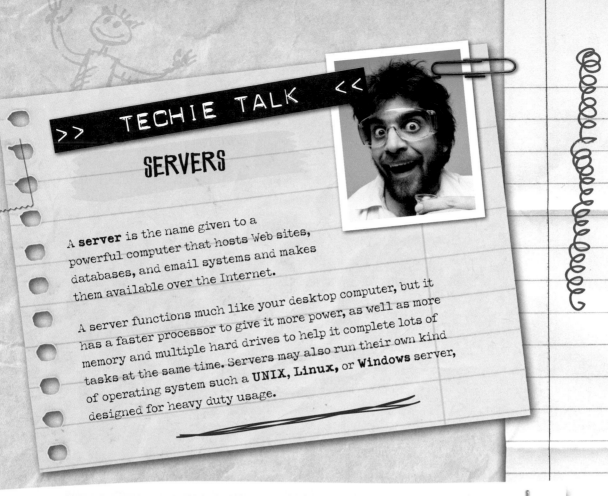

SERVERS

A **server** is the name given to a powerful computer that hosts Web sites, databases, and email systems and makes them available over the Internet.

A server functions much like your desktop computer, but it has a faster processor to give it more power, as well as more memory and multiple hard drives to help it complete lots of tasks at the same time. Servers may also run their own kind of operating system such a **UNIX**, **Linux**, or **Windows** server, designed for heavy duty usage.

✳ HOW DOES A BROWSER FIND MY WEB SITE?

When you type a Web address into your browser, your computer locates that Web site wherever it is in the world and brings back the pages to display. Most of us have trouble remembering where our house keys are, so how on earth does a browser find a single Web site among the millions available online?

The answer is that Web sites and the computers that host them have names, just like people. However, rather than being called Bill or Sally, every Web site has a name that is visible to browsers and known as a **URL**: for example, www.myWeb site.co.uk. Every server also has a name, known as an **IP Address**, which is usually a number such as 192.88.12.9. The user-friendly URL serves as a reference for your computer to the IP address of the server on which the Web site files are held. It also tells your computer the exact location of the Web site files on that server.

Uniform Resource Locator

Internet Protocol Address

DNS for short

All these names are recorded by the **Domain Name System**. The Domain Name System was developed by **Sun Microsystems** in the early 1980s as a convenient way to keep track of all these names by recording them on servers specially designed for this purpose.

There are a lot of Web pages in the world, so the DNS files them in a vast directory. A simple way to think of it is like an army with generals at the top and soldiers at the bottom. Each top-level, or primary, domain (the generals) maintains a list of the subordinate, or secondary, domains beneath it (the captains). The secondary domains hold lists containing IP addresses for every Web site (the soldiers). This hierarchy means any Web address can be located, because every DNS server in the chain knows about all other DNS servers beneath it.

✳ URLS

A URL is composed of various elements that tell the browser what it should be looking for and where. This is usually a Web page, but it could be a text document, some graphics, or a program. An example of a URL might be:

network protocol – this tells the browser how the data is going to be transferred across the Internet, for example http://ftp:// or mailto://

domain suffix – this is information about the top-level domain

http://www.**quickexpert**.co.uk/**books/default.html**

host name or address – this identifies who owns the Web site and where they are, for example "quickexpert"

file or resource location – this is where to find the individual Web page you want on the computer that hosts it, for example /document/index.html

Full URLs featuring all four substrings are called absolute URLs, because they contain all the information you need to find a page from anywhere on the Web.

In some cases, URLs will only contain the file or resource location because they are only used to move around within Web sites. These are called relative URLs.

"Be nice to nerds. Chances are you'll end up working for one."

Bill Gates,
founder of Microsoft

SAY WHAT?

QUICK EXPERT SUMMARY

- ◉ The Internet is more than 40 years old.

- ◉ The Internet is used to communicate all kinds of digital data not just Web sites.

- ◉ The World Wide Web is a network of Web sites connected by hyperlinks across the Internet.

- ◉ Hyptertext was invented by the British scientist Tim Berners-Lee.

- ◉ Web sites are hosted on powerful computers called servers.

- ◉ Each Web site has its own name known as a URL.

- ◉ A URL contains information about where to find a particular page on the Web.

☀ Taking it further

The great thing about the Internet is that it is designed for everybody to use, free of charge. The vision of Tim Berners Lee and the other founding fathers of the Web was that their new online world should be open for all to access and all to contribute to. We've seen how easy it is to create Web pages and just how they can be used to present words, graphics, photographs, video, and audio. So, what's the next step?

The writer Charles Caleb Colton once said that "imitation is the sincerest [form] of flattery," but we know it is also the quickest way to learn. Now that you are a quick expert, make a list of your ten favorite Web sites. Take another look at them and ask yourself a few questions:

Q How have the creators of these Web sites laid out text and graphics to make them easy to read?

Q How have they used colors that go together well to create a professional look and feel?

Q How have they laid out their pages to group content into easy-to-understand themes?

Q Which interactive elements work well and why?

Q Finally, we learned just how easy it is to peek at the code; is there anything on these Web sites that you could borrow and add to yours?

By keeping an eye on what you think has worked well on other Web sites, you will be able to extend your skills easily and build on these ideas to make them even better. Who knows, before long another quick expert might be looking at your Web site and thinking, "How did they do that?"

app Sort for "application;" a program that performs a task on a computer or other digital device.

attribute Additional information describing the use of a tag or style element.

browser A program that is used to view Web pages.

cloud Computing services delivered online in a virtual environment.

code A set of instructions for a computer; a system of signals or symbols for communication.

comment Code that makes the browser ignore styling.

console An electronic system that connects to a display (such as a television set) and is used primarily to play video games; a combination of readouts or displays and an input device (such as a keyboard) by which an operator can monitor and interact with a system (such as a computer).

container tag An HTML tag used in pairs and wrapped around content.

CSS Short for Cascading Style Sheets; a coding language that is used to define the style and look of a Web page.

DNS Stands for Domain Name System; an Internet system that translates names into IP addresses.

empty tag An HTML tag that stands alone.

FTP Short for File Transfer Protocol; a system that is used to transfer files from one computer to another via a network, such as the Internet.

GIF Stands for Graphic Interchange Format, a digital image format that also supports animation.

hexadecimal color Numerical representation of color used in HTML.

HTML Stands for Hypertext Mark-Up Language, the main language used for displaying Web pages and other information in a Web browser.

HTML editor A program that is used to browse and write HTML.

HTTP Short for Hypertext Transfer Protocol, the system that allows data to be exchanged on the World Wide Web.

hypertext The name given to content created in HTML.

IA Stands for information architecture, the way in which a Web site's Web pages are organized and structured.

Internet A global network of connected computers.

IP address Short for Internet Protocol address, the unique number each device connected to a network has.

JPEG Stands for Joint Photographic Experts Group, a common digital image format.

MAILTO A system used to transfer emails within a network.

multimedia Images, video, sounds, and text combined on the Web.

network A system of computers. peripherals, terminals, and databases connected by communication lines; an interconnected or interrelated chain, group, or system.

online Connected to, served by, or available through a system, especially a computer or telecommunications system (such as the Internet).

open source Free software developed and maintained online.

PNG Stands for Portable Network Graphic, a common format for a digital image.

server A computer that is connected to the Internet and hosts Web sites.

software The entire set of programs, procedures, and related documentation associated with a system, especially a computer system; computer programs.

style sheet A text document that gives a browser information about the design of a Web site.

TAG A piece of code that gives direction to a browser in HTML.

TCP/IP Stands for Transmission Control Protocol/Internet Protocol; a system which allows "packets" of data to be transmitted between computers connected to the same network.

URL Short for Uniform Resource Locator, a string of characters that functions as the address for a Web site or document on the Internet.

usability The degree to which a Web site is user-friendly and easy to navigate.

WC3 The World Wide Web Consortium; a community of individuals and organizations that work together to develop Web standards. Its members include Tim Berners-Lee, the inventor of the World Wide Web.

Web page A text file written in HTML.

Web site A collection of Web pages held under one URL.

widget Reusable code or tools that can be added to a Web site.

WWW Short for the World Wide Web, a system of interlinked documents that is accessed via the Internet.

Get Net Wise
Internet Education Foundation
1634 I Street, NW
Washington DC 20009
Web site: http://www.getnetwise
.org
Get Net Wise is part of the
Internet Education
Foundation, which works
to provide a safe online
environment for children and
families.

Internet Keep Safe Coalition
1401 K Street NW, Suite 600
Washington, DC 20005
(866) 794-7233
Web site: http://www.ikeepsafe
.org

The Internet Keep Safe Coalition
is an educational resource
for children and families
that educates about
Internet safety and ethics
associated with Internet
technologies.

The Internet Society (ISOC)
1775 Wiehle Avenue, Suite 201
Reston, VA 20190-5108
(703) 439-2120
Web site: http://www.isoc.org
The ISOC is a nonprofit
organization that
concentrates on maintaining
high standards for Internet
infrastructure and promotes
education and government

policies that promote open
online environments.

i-SAFE Inc.
5900 Pasteur Court, Suite #100
Carlsbad, CA 92008
(760) 603-7911
Web site: http://www.isafe.org
i-SAFE is a nonprofit foundation
    whose mission is to educate
    and empower youth to make
    their Internet experiences safe
    and responsible. The goal is
    to educate students on how to
    avoid dangerous, inappropriate,
    or unlawful online behavior.

NetSmartz
Charles B. Wang
    International Children's Building
699 Prince Street

Alexandria, VA 22314-3175
(800) 843-5678
Web site: http://www.netsmartz.org
NetSmartz provides children, teens,
    and parents resources to help
    educate young people about
    how to surf the Internet safely.

>> WEB SITES <<

Due to the changing nature of
Internet links, Rosen Publishing
has developed an online list of Web
sites related to the subject of this
book. This site is updated regularly.
Please use this link to access
the list:

http://www.rosenlinks.com/QEG/Webs